This journal belongs to

Class starts Monday Oct 26 2020

I offer myself now to the creator now as a channel

I offer myself now to the creator as a channel

I offer myself now to the creator as a channel

Dr Rhonda Marie Gibson and Diesel Gibson Owner Directors Spiritual Advisors

Opening 2022

The Institute of Quantum Light Energy Healing and of Harmony

Travel Travel Travel

Mivo — Wice'ktown Healing Centre, World Wide.

Healing Facility

Stylized
WORKBOOKS

Action in the world is part of my soul's purpose and plan.

Ask the Mother of Mercy to bless it into Resolution

do not control ~~of~~

~~Thoughtfully~~ **Stylized** Pray

WORKBOOKS Carefully

Pray

Pray

manipulate situations (Pray)

for such actions are unworthy of my magnitude and are unnecessary for my success.

My prayers are powerful

Nicholas Susilas
my dearest guide
please hel

Just for today I will not
worry Just for today
I will not be angry
Just for today I will
be greatful
Today is my little Alices
birthday she is 4
who is with her mother
Devon is sad he is
drinking No Judgement
Andrea is here I am
so greatful Devon and
her are here.
No Anger,
    Just for today I will
be kind to every
living thing
I have never I seen
more beautifuly
I hear more sweetly
I love more passionatly

today to counsel or 4
came to me and laughed
Dee sel and I
yesterday I asked for
1 Billion dollars for
my Bracelt I did 2
metatims + com Brian Scott
I still did not finish
his video's they are
amazing
1) the magical you withsten
2) one on money
I did not ask for money
for me I am so greatful for
what I have and that I
really have what I need
money to buy the sels
and get whatever I want
everything. I do not
need anything else I can
take care of the kids
and pay for everything
I need and more mom
always helps there
is money everywhere

now that I have
forgiven my
concious unconcious
and csupenonurers cself
WOW feels so good
I carry nothing I had
to to serve Spirit God
Creator, the Counsel
of 9. I could not
be a victim any longer
I was cocouning now
I am the butterfly
Sept 27, 2020
9 + 4 -
13 - (4)
I am healer
4 = ArchAngels
Mercury
Uranus
Satur
Emperor
Green
stabulzer
self sacrifie

aware and accepting
yesterday I became
aware and accepting
of all my mistakes
my miss steps.
past mistakes misconception
most of them had to
do w/the Devon and
I am so very sorry
I tried and did
the best I could do
at the time. I am going
to do better every second
of the rest of my
life. I go back in
time and change every
second of what I
feel guilty and ashamed
for and change those
scene to only
pure unconditional ~~thoughl~~
light and love

I am not scared at all about this next project (Mindset or Harmony) I am so excited I am so Blessed my soul and my ~~aura~~ avatar are so so so so so so excited. Devon Andrea and Diesel are excellent soul partners my soul tribe, my twin flame, soul mates, △ we are the three. We are ready I am ready Today is day One. The journey begins

My Cards:
1) Metron
2) Lumi°
3) blessed Be.

4) metrion
5) spult
7) Ascended Master

Cards counsel of 9 asking
me to draw from for
the Beginning of my journey

Why write - important why card
important

1). how do they talk to
me telaphatically
2). So others know
3) so others see

Very specific question

Tell we where to begin

(Reading)

1) Metatron Oracle
Light
   live in light
   connects to source
   you are divine light
   the light is always
   shining within and
around you
Become light
   let it shine through you
Gift light
You are love
You are divine light
   feel this each
day you are awake

(L I G H T)

2) Rumi

44

Merciful Mother Jamal

O Sudden Resurrection
O countless Blessings
O Blazing Fire
in the Jungle of thought
Today you arrive w/ laughter
in Breaking open the jail
Rumi.

You cannot fail

you are being asked to
take stock of your
thoughts and attitudes

Having to be tough and play

hard ball has served its
purpose, yet this oracle

comes to you w/ the

guidance to become
softer in your
way and
attitudes.

Can you gently
but firmly place
to one side the
judge within
the one who keeps
score

and demands retribution
an eye for an eye. The
exponent of absolute
justice? Can you
invite instead the
one who gentles the
aggressive lodged within
and allows him to bow
before the great
lady who loves, is
wise, and who

Steadies the working
of the world with
the softest of touches

Do not worry

You are strong
enough now
to become gentle

If you have to
fight ask for the
Mother of Mercy to
bless it unto

resolution

to

My prayers are powerful
Although action in the
world is part of
my soul's purpose
and plan , when
I pray, I must
have conviction that
my prayers are
real , are heard

and are responded to
by the great universal
heart. Pray
Carefully and
thoughtfully
Ritual

(3) Ascended Masters
The 7th Ray
The Violet Ray
Ray Of
Transmutation

Institute "Now" the
Establishment of
the Seventh Golden
Age of harmony
Peace, beauty,
abundance, perfection,
and true Brotherhood,
through the path of

the love of your own
heart flame"
Master Saint Germain"

I am a being of
the violet fire
I am the flame
of God's desire

Soul Chakra

Gift of the

Holy Spirit

Prophecy and

the Holy Spirit
and the working
of miracles

The cave of Symbols
Table Mountain
Wyoming USA
The Temple of
the Maltese Cross

Vibration Purple
Pink Aqua Teal

Gemstone Amethyst
Diamond Aquamarine

Qualities Freedom
Alchemy
Justice
Diplomacy
Transmutation
Ray Saturday

embodied by prophet
Samuel, St Joseph
St Alban, Merlin, Roger
Bacon, Christopher Columbus
Sir Francis Bacon

On the Sabbath of
the Seventh Ray,
you greet the Master
of the Aquarian Age:

Saint Germain, friend of
old, I am honoured at
they presence here! So may I
know the so cosmic honour flame
that is entwined with strands
of gold and violet as
elements weave a
garland of garland

of praise to the
Knight Commander
of my heart." And
you tarry before the
alchemest of the
Spirit who has come
who has come to
track you, the science
of the ~~amathyst~~
the amethyst ray
and the ritual
of grace

that will be the law

for the next 200 years'

(5) Blessed Be

A Blessing of the Waters
Pouring

Clean and Purify
Rebirth and Restore
Forgiveness

remove the dark
memories we
dwell on
intelligence of fear

May you never thirst
and always be blessed
by water
Blessed Be

5 Dolphin ~~Spirit~~

A magical journey
begins as 2 play
in the world
Spirit of happiness

Captivating, infectious
see the good in everyone
bring out the best in
everyone →
make people want to
join them
Playing = happiness
Playing = connecting
to others
Dolphin Spirit =
Water Spirit

= Sacredness Flow Trace

= Sacredness of all life

= animals, planets, elementals

highest and noblest

of activities

Play — used it
always often
with others, connection

life then becomes

a celebration of
each moment with
others

Healing Power Of
WATER
SOUND BEAUTY

(6) Becon
Shine On

(44) Master Number

Energy linked
to the Angles
and I am an earth
angel

I am a becon of
Light in this
world. a place
of refuge fim
the storm a
port for the
Storm =
(Harmony)

So many drowning because
they find no one signaling
a way HOME

many in need

I ASK HOW WhereWHEN?

JUST SHINE
It will Be NOTiced
YOU NEED to be NOTICED
TO STAND OUT
DO IT OR DO NOT

This is my role
My MISSION IS
HARMONY

Shine Your Light

music

While

Me Havese

me

Buan Scott

uses

Conclusion

began with
Light
ended Light

Energy to
linked
angels
masters
earth
angels
everything
breathes
spheres

Light is
harmony is
frequencies
Beame the light — love
Merciful Mother Jamal
Soft = gentlee, wise
prayer powerful
Ascended Master
33 Germain
abundance

Being
Powerful
Master human

Water
Spirit
release trust past Peace
Dolphin
happiness
Play the people
healing power the
people ok

The love of
your own
Heart Alchemy
healing power
of connecting

Flame
healing power
of water

Play Animals
Planet

merka
dal e

merkaba
con gure

silver
fs

△ △ △   ☿
amathst

                    Red
        Amathyst   Jasper
st Germain   fs

                         tromaline
                         fs

        silver
        gold
platonic bronze /copper
solids

chir
in
Tigers

model
string

Bracelet

purple

material

(clasp)

small

bed

Nicolas Tesla
my dearest guide
please join my
deepest self
tonight and help
me create the
uius bracelet
in my sleep

please meet
me and show
me so I can
see how it is
do

Remember it
and write
it down

Tomorrow
Morning

rope
beads
chain

Sept 29   not bracelet

necklace

Back   purple
              silver
              red

              black

Metation's
cube
an back

Rope - Black

silver

Back
Metatrons
cube

red

copper

Red

gold
silver

Black   Purple

copper
silver

heal properties
of copper

Venus
final

necklace

red

square
silver
purple

I live everyone on the planet

Black

copper

& Circle
gold

Back

metatronic cube

Black rope

I have asked my guardian angel for the money to help get this off the ground

1 billion dollars

done

Now I need a prototype

Oct 1st/2020
full moon

2   9 day exercises
every 3 hours
Council of 9

frequency (projection
(gratitude)
purlict
actim
feel joy

Galactic meditation
(copy)

plus 9 day prayer
for family

hologram

Marina Jalali

new earth newversion

render blueprint
after first 3 days

4—5 6th   galactic
every (2 hrs)   meditation

7—8 9

— every hour

New
earth
meditation

Oct 2/ 2020

Day 2
for Marina's
meditation beautiful
powerful, Austan
you felt like my
very good friend ☺
family soul
healing deep gratitude
Diesel we are all
good
healing quantum
♡ Donald — ☺☺

Oct 4/2020

0   Zero Point
1 =   Circle   ✓
2 =   Vesica Pisces
3 =   Triangle   ✓
4 =   Square
5   Pentagram
6   Merkaba   ✓
7   Heptogram
8

I S.

I c o sahedron   water

heaven dodecahedron

air — octohedron

cube

Manufactured by Amazon.ca
Bolton, ON